The Council of Europe's
Common European Framework

B1 level

the
vocabulary
files

English Usage

Intermediate

GlobalELT
ENGLISH LANGUAGE TEACHING BOOKS

Vocabulary Files
CEF Level B1

Published by GLOBAL ELT LTD
www.globalelt.co.uk
email: orders@globalelt.co.uk
Copyright © **GLOBAL ELT LTD**

The right of Lawrence Mamas & Andrew Betsis to be identified as the authors
of this work has been asserted in accordance with the Copyright, Designs and Patent Act 1988.

All rights reserved. No part of this publication may be reproduced, stored in a retrieval system, or transmitted in any form or by any means, electronic, mechanical, photocopying, recording or otherwise, without the prior permission in writing of the Publisher. Any person who does any unauthorised act in relation to this publication may be liable to criminal prosecution and civil claims for damages.

British Library Cataloguing-in-Publication Data

Components:
- Vocabulary Files - Level B1- Teacher's Book - ISBN: 978-1-904663-42-3
- Vocabulary Files - Level B1- Student's Book - ISBN: 978-1-904663-41-6

CONTENTS

Unit		Page
Unit 1	WORK	4
Unit 2	DESCRIBING THINGS	8
Unit 3	THE MEDIA	12
Unit 4	PREDICTIONS	16
Unit 5	ANIMALS	20
Unit 6	SOCIALISING	24
Unit 7	CELEBRATIONS & CULTURE	28
Unit 8	CLOTHES	32
Unit 9	FAMILY & MARRIAGE	36
Unit 10	LETTERS	40
Unit 11	TRAVEL	44
Unit 12	COOKERY	48
Unit 13	PEOPLE	52
Unit 14	THE SEA	56
Unit 15	SPORTS & FITNESS	60

work

EXERCISE 1

Below are 12 words which are all somehow connected with the world of work. Put the words into two groups and then give each group of words a title.

clerk   computer   businessman   printer   telephone
colleague   secretary   manager   FAX machine
typewriter   director   answering machine

A: Office Workers	B: Office Equipment
clerk	computer
businessman	printer
colleague	telephone
secretary	fax machine
manager	typewriter
director	answering machine

EXERCISE 2

Match the following words which are related to each other in different ways:

1 earn   [3] colleague
2 salary   [5] office
3 workmate   [1] win
4 job   [2] wage
5 factory   [4] work

EXERCISE 3

> ☞ The words 'earn' and 'win' are often confused by students.
> **to earn** = to get money by working; to get paid for a job, e.g. *earn money*
> **to win** = 1 to gain victory in a game, contest, etc, e.g. *win a match*
> 2 to obtain a prize in a competition etc, often by luck
> e.g. *He won £50 in the crossword competition.*

Show that you understand the relationship and the difference between the pairs of words from EXERCISE 2 by completing the following grid with their correct forms:

PAIR OF WORDS	EXAMPLES
wage **salary**	Factory workers are paid a weekly __wage__ . Teachers are being offered __salaries__ of over £15,000 a year.
job **work**	I had a part-time __job__ as a gardener when I was a student. Coalminers __work__ in dangerous and unpleasant conditions.
earn **win**	He doesn't __earn__ enough to support his family. If I __win__ the lottery, I'll buy you a car.
factory **office**	Workers at the car __factory__ complained about the noise of the new machinery. The lawyer's __office__ is on the third floor.
workmate **colleague**	He sometimes went for a drink after work with his __workmates__ from the building site. She discussed with her __colleague(s)__ the possibility of a promotion to senior manager.

EXERCISE 4

In recent years, there has been a fashion for starting small businesses, e.g. small restaurants, services or shops. It takes a lot of courage and usually some financial aid in the form of a bank loan to set up your own business. It means taking a risk, too, because you can never be sure if your business will be a success. You could find yourself owing a lot of money to the bank, or, in the worst of circumstances, you could even 'go bust'.
On the other hand, you could earn a good living if you are prepared to work hard — who knows? You could even become a millionaire!

Match the following verbs and noun phrases to form expressions which appear in the text:

1. to set up
2. to take
3. to be
4. to go
5. to earn

[5] a living
[4] bust
[1] a business
[2] a risk
[3] a success

EXERCISE 5 — Word building

Complete the following grid with the correct form of the words:

VERB	NOUN	ADJECTIVE
succeed	success	successful
live	life, living	lively
risk	risk	risky
manage	manager/management	manageable
encourage	courage	courageous/encouraging

Now use the information above to fill the gaps in these sentences:

1. My parents __encouraged__ me to train as an accountant.
2. The shop's __manager__ locks up at the end of the day.
3. You can't get rich without taking a few __risks__.
4. I took the exam but unfortunately I wasn't __successful__.
5. My grandfather __lived__ to the age of ninety-eight.

EXERCISE 6

Frequently confused words

Fill the gaps in the sentences below with the correct forms of the words in the box:

| lend | owe | borrow | debt | loan |

Usage note:
In BrE the word 'loan' has only ever really been used as a noun except occasionally in specialist areas such as banking. In AmE 'loan' has long been used as a verb. This usage is becoming more common in BrE today.

1 I ____borrowed____ a romantic novel from the library.

2 I'm going to ask my father for a ____loan____ of £500 so I can buy a motorbike. Do you think he'll agree?

3 If I ____lend / loan____ you this shirt I know I'll never get it back in one piece.

4 I've spent so much money this month, I'll soon be running into ____debt____.

5 I'm still waiting for you to give me back that fiver you ____owe____ me.

EXERCISE 7

Work-related vocabulary

*The words in the box below can be combined with the word **work**. Sort them into two groups, those which can precede and those which can follow 'work':*

| house | man | load | home | paper | force |
| brick | book | top | over | | |

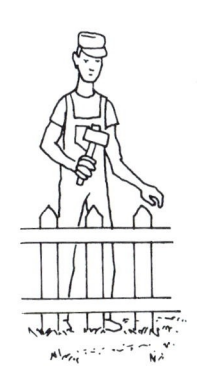

_____ work	work _____
housework	workman
homework	workload
paperwork	workforce
brickwork	worktop
overwork	workbook

Now complete the following sentences with the correct compound:

1 A *work* **man** arrived yesterday to put up a new fence.

2 Many women complain that their husbands don't do any **house** *work*.

3 Employees are demanding higher wages to compensate for their increased *work* **load**.

4 For your ____**home***work*____, complete Exercise 10 in your *work* **book**.

7

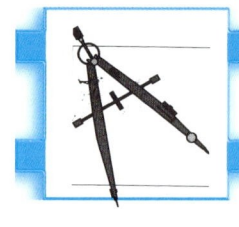

describing things

ADJECTIVES	
big	small
large	little
huge	tiny
enormous	minute

EXERCISE 1

Match the words with similar meaning in the list below:

1 big

2 small

3 minute

4 new

5 round

[5] circular

[3] tiny

[4] modern

[1] large

[2] little

Now match the words with opposite meanings below:

1 old

2 heavy

3 tiny

4 brand new

5 antique

[2] light

[5] modern

[4] second-hand

[3] huge

[1] new

8

Unit 2 Describing

EXERCISE 2

Use the words from the previous exercises to complete the sentences below:

1 This isn't __brand new__ ; it's second-hand.

2 They have a modern house but it's full of __antique__ furniture.

3 This pile of books is too __heavy__ to carry. Could you help me?

4 She used to live in a tiny flat in Battersea, but after the success of her book she moved to a __huge__ house with eleven rooms.

5 Do you prefer square or __round__ clock-faces?

6 This blouse comes in three sizes: small, medium and __large__ .

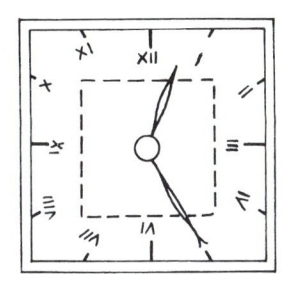

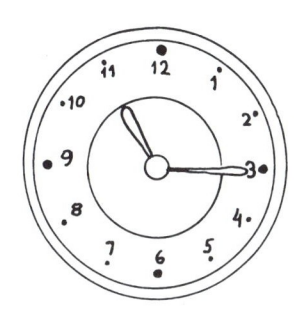

EXERCISE 3

The following denote particles or small quantities of things. Match the words on the left with those on the right to form phrases:

1	a grain of		1	sand
2	a crumb of		7	light
3	a spoonful of		8	paper
4	a bouquet of		5	water
5	a drop of		6	salt
6	a pinch of		3	medicine
7	a ray of		2	bread
8	a scrap of		9	hair
9	a lock of		4	flowers

EXERCISE 4

Fill the gaps in the following sentences with words from the previous exercise in their correct forms:

1 I wrote my address down on a ___scrap___ of ___paper___.

2 The recipe says you should add a ___pinch___ of ___salt___ to the sauce.

3 I enjoyed the picnic on the beach but I kept getting ___grains___ of ___sand___ in my sandwiches.

4 I felt a ___drop___ of ___water___ on my head; it must be starting to rain.

5 He's so romantic; he sent me a huge ___bouquet___ of ___flowers___ on Valentine's Day.

EXERCISE 5

Describing objects

We often derive the name of something from the purpose for which it is intended. For example, a **jam jar** *is a jar which is used or has been used as a container for jam. Match the following nouns in a similar way:*

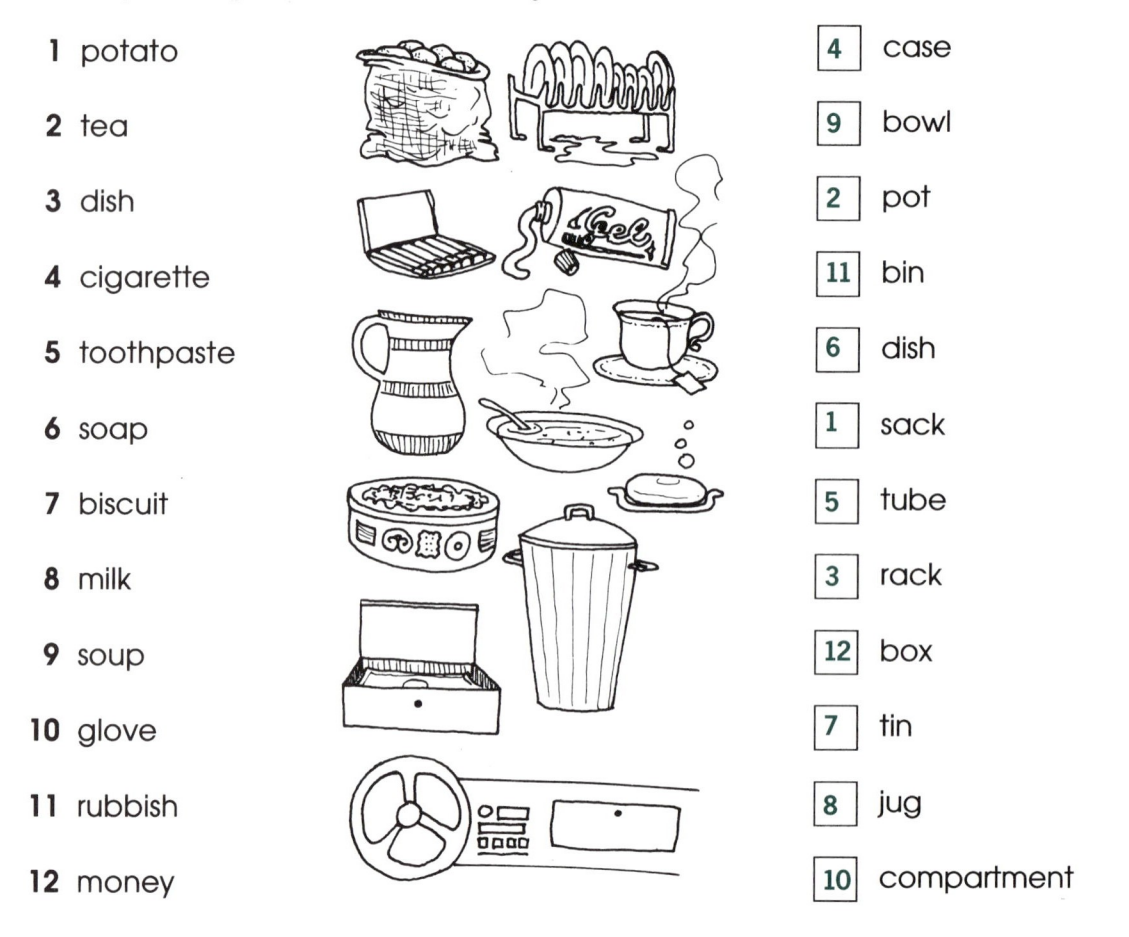

1	potato		4	case
2	tea		9	bowl
3	dish		2	pot
4	cigarette		11	bin
5	toothpaste		6	dish
6	soap		1	sack
7	biscuit		5	tube
8	milk		3	rack
9	soup		12	box
10	glove		7	tin
11	rubbish		8	jug
12	money		10	compartment

EXERCISE 6

Choose from the words in the box to complete the sentences below:

| synthetic | delicious | refreshing | stylish | skilful | dramatic |

1 That was a really __delicious__ meal!

2 I enjoyed the play; the murder scene was very __dramatic__.

3 My shirt is made of __synthetic__ material but I would prefer cotton.

4 Lemonade is a very __refreshing__ drink in the summertime.

5 You have to be a pretty __skilful__ driver to cope with those sharp bends on the coastal road.

6 She wore a very __stylish__ outfit to the wedding.

EXERCISE 7

Find 18 adjectives from this unit in the wordsearch square below:

enormous	synthetic	delicious	stylish	large	minute	huge
round	antique	new	heavy	tiny	small
big	little	old	dark	modern

E	T	U	N	I	M	N	E	W	D
N	I	Z	Y	L	I	T	T	L	E
O	N	R	V	T	E	G	R	A	L
R	Y	A	A	F	D	L	O	D	I
M	O	D	E	R	N	W	U	A	C
O	S	J	H	U	G	E	N	R	I
U	B	S	M	A	L	L	D	K	O
S	Y	N	T	H	E	T	I	C	U
X	G	M	H	S	I	L	Y	T	S
A	N	T	I	Q	U	E	B	I	G

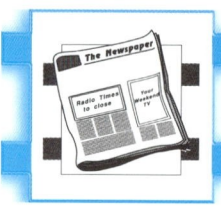

the media

> The **media** are the means of mass communication, e.g. television, radio, newspapers. Their purpose is to entertain or spread news and information to a large number of people.

EXERCISE 1

Sort the following vocabulary items into two groups:
words associated with newspapers *and* words associated with television.

article   programme   presenter   reader   viewer
print   channel   press   show   headline

NEWSPAPERS	TELEVISION
article	programme
reader	presenter
print	viewer
press	channel
headline	show

EXERCISE 2

Look at the diagram of the front page of a daily newspaper and label the following parts:

1 front page
2 picture
3 paragraph
4 column
5 headline

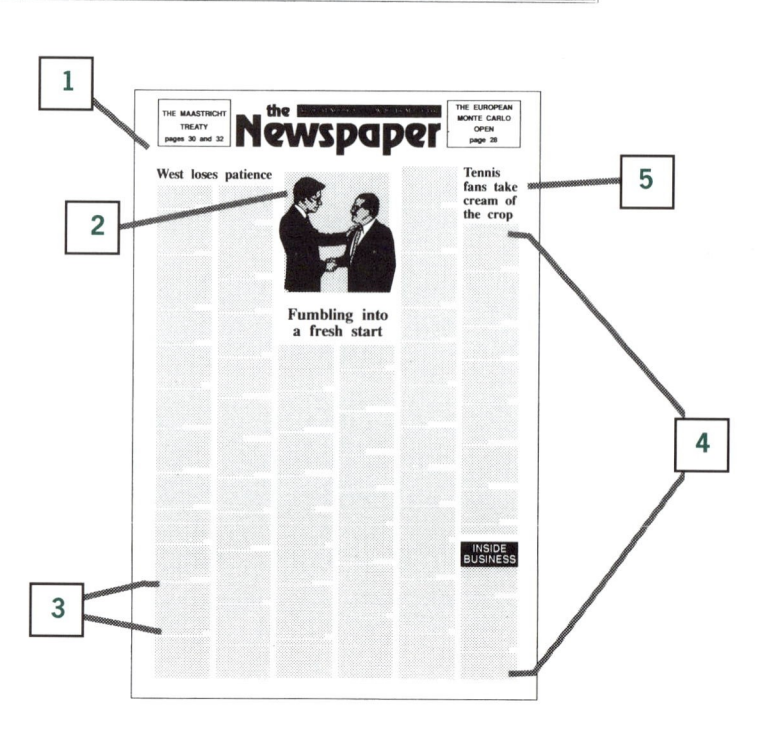

Unit 3 The Media

EXERCISE 3

Now complete the following sentences with the words in the previous exercise in their correct forms:

1 The lead(ing) story appears on the __front page__ .

2 The __headline__ captures the reader's attention and introduces him or her to the topic of the main story.

3 Each article is printed down the page in __columns__ .

4 A __picture__ provides vitality and can make the events in the news seem more immediate to the reader.

5 A news article is divided into __paragraphs__ so that it's easier to read.

EXERCISE 4

Match the following terms with the correct definition from the choices given below:

> the editor   a journalist   an illustrator
> a correspondent   the Press

1 Someone who collects information for and writes news articles

  is __a journalist__

2 The person who provides the sketches and cartoons for the newspaper

  is __an illustrator__

3 A collective term for certain media personnel

  is __the Press__

4 The person who decides on the overall policy and content of the newspaper

  is __the editor__

5 A reporter working on a news story on the spot, e.g. in a foreign country,

  is __a correspondent__

EXERCISE 5

Example Answers - variations possible.

*The purpose of a **headline** is to sum up in a few words the main news event. Read the following imaginary newspaper headlines and write them out in full sentences:*

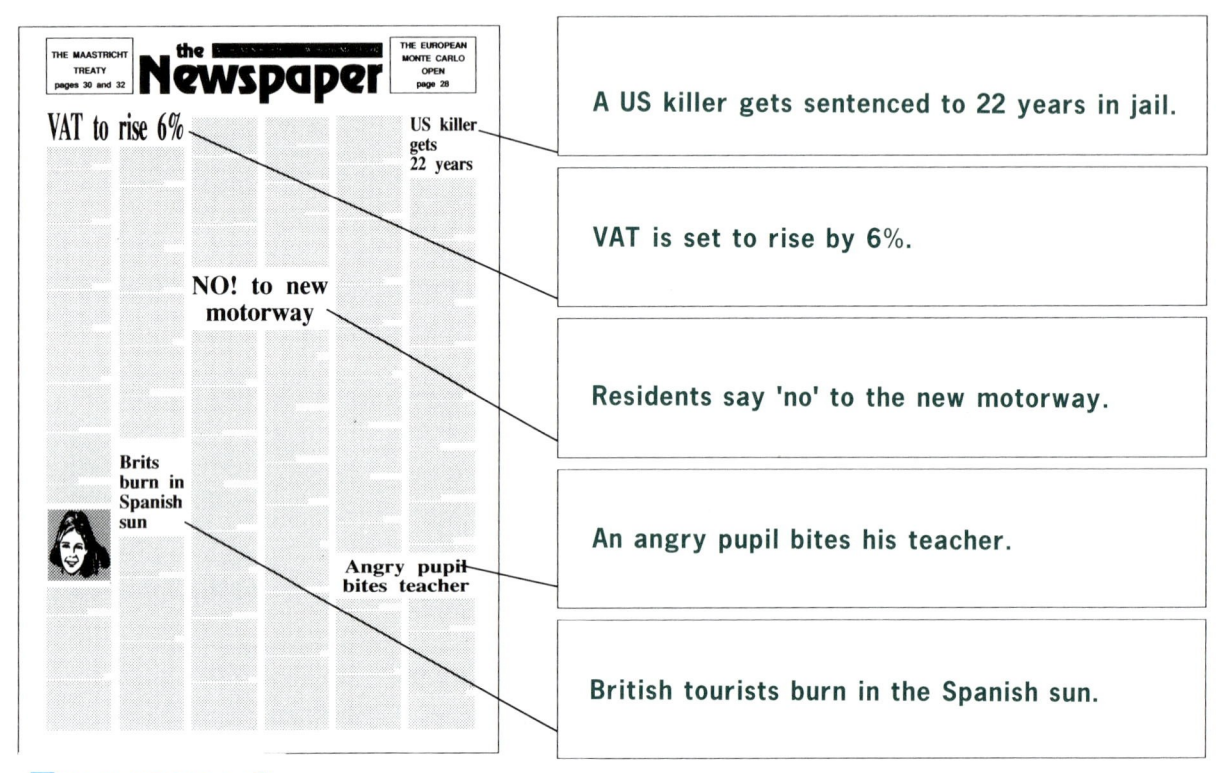

A US killer gets sentenced to 22 years in jail.

VAT is set to rise by 6%.

Residents say 'no' to the new motorway.

An angry pupil bites his teacher.

British tourists burn in the Spanish sun.

EXERCISE 6

☞ Newspapers and television have a strong influence on the ideas and opinions of the general public. However, we rely on the media as a whole to provide us with entertainment as well as information.

Can you match the definitions with the following types of TV show?

| quiz show   game show   talk show |
| series/serial   soap opera |

1 An interviewer (the host) talks to different celebrities each week, often with a studio audience present.

1. talk show

2 On-going television drama whose storyline claims to reflect issues and happenings of everyday life.

2. soap opera

3 Individuals or teams answer general knowledge questions to win cash or other prizes.

3. quiz show

14

4 Television drama divided into a number of episodes and broadcast at regular weekly times.   4. series/serial

5 Individuals or teams take part in activities to win cash or other prizes.   5. game show

Into which category of television show do you think the following fall?

Coronation Street	soap opera
Wheel of Fortune	game show
Lost	series/serial
Who wants to be a millionaire?	quiz show
The Larry King Show	talk show

EXERCISE 7 Research

Go to a newsagent's or kiosk which sells foreign magazines and newspapers and find British examples of the following:

Example Answer: Students should write their own.

1 a women's magazine — Hello!
2 a sports magazine — Shoot
3 a daily newspaper — The Times
4 a music magazine/newspaper — Q Magazine
5 a computer magazine — Computer Weekly

15

predictions

EXERCISE 1

Horoscopes

☞ **Astrology** is just one of the many ways which people use to try to find out what is going to happen in the future. Can you match the signs of the zodiac with their Latin names?

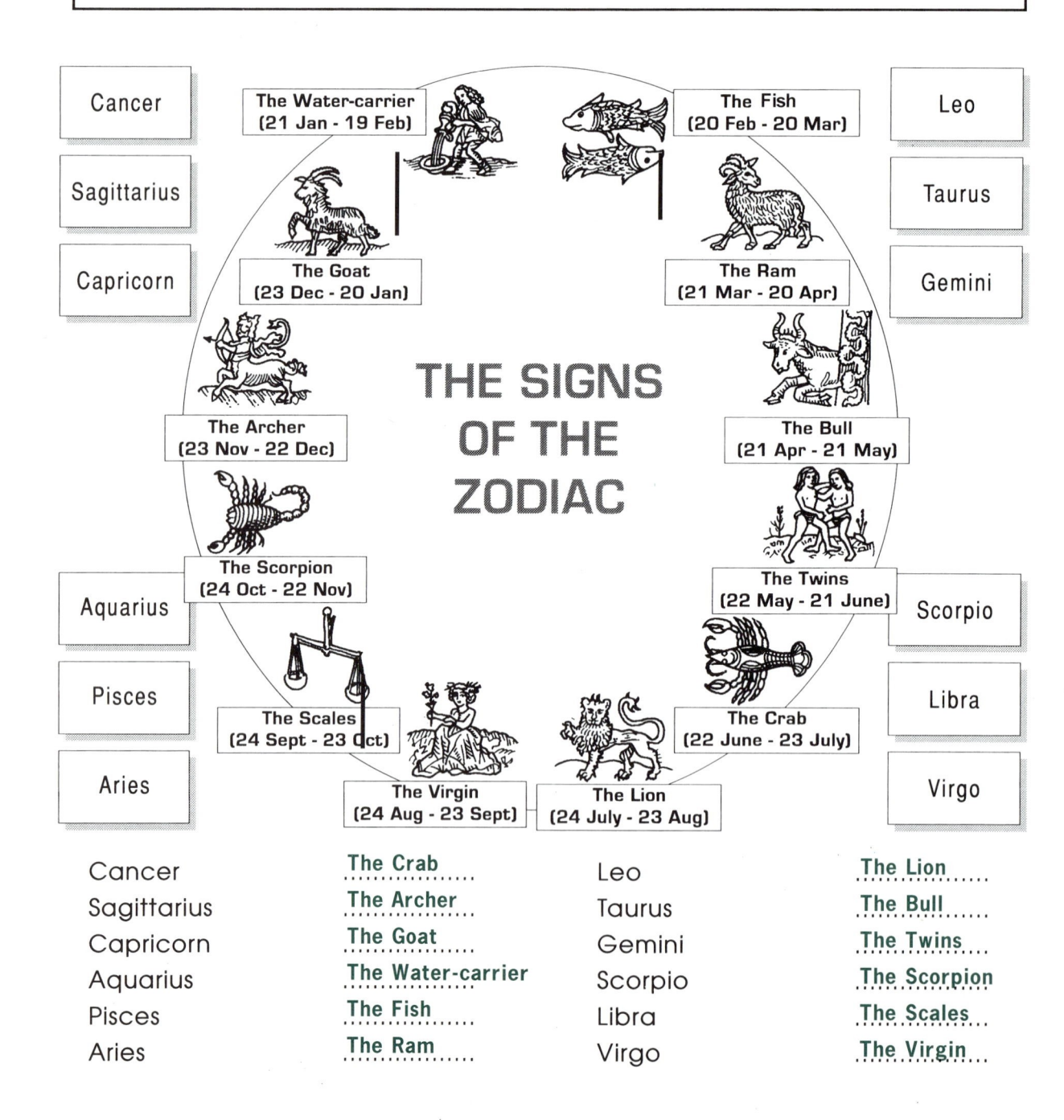

THE SIGNS OF THE ZODIAC

- Cancer
- Sagittarius
- Capricorn
- Aquarius
- Pisces
- Aries

- The Water-carrier (21 Jan - 19 Feb)
- The Fish (20 Feb - 20 Mar)
- The Goat (23 Dec - 20 Jan)
- The Ram (21 Mar - 20 Apr)
- The Archer (23 Nov - 22 Dec)
- The Bull (21 Apr - 21 May)
- The Scorpion (24 Oct - 22 Nov)
- The Twins (22 May - 21 June)
- The Scales (24 Sept - 23 Oct)
- The Crab (22 June - 23 July)
- The Virgin (24 Aug - 23 Sept)
- The Lion (24 July - 23 Aug)

- Leo
- Taurus
- Gemini
- Scorpio
- Libra
- Virgo

Cancer	The Crab	Leo	The Lion
Sagittarius	The Archer	Taurus	The Bull
Capricorn	The Goat	Gemini	The Twins
Aquarius	The Water-carrier	Scorpio	The Scorpion
Pisces	The Fish	Libra	The Scales
Aries	The Ram	Virgo	The Virgin

EXERCISE 2

☞ If you believe that certain things are signs of bad luck and that others are signs of good luck, you are said to be **superstitious.**

Some superstitions involve everyday incidents. Do you know whether the following are considered omens of good or bad luck? Tick the right column.

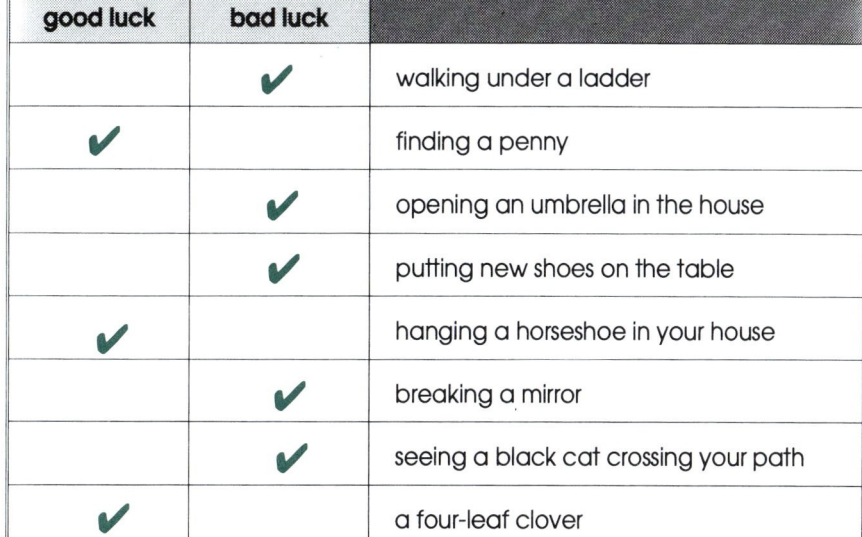

good luck	bad luck	
	✔	walking under a ladder
✔		finding a penny
	✔	opening an umbrella in the house
	✔	putting new shoes on the table
✔		hanging a horseshoe in your house
	✔	breaking a mirror
	✔	seeing a black cat crossing your path
✔		a four-leaf clover

Can you think of any more superstitions? Do you think they should be taken seriously?

EXERCISE 3

The following are expressions connected with luck. Can you match the expression with the situation in which it is used?

1 Break a leg!

2 Beginner's luck.

3 Best of luck.

4 Better luck next time.

5 A lucky escape.

3	*When someone is going to take an exam, go to an interview, start a new job, etc.*
1	*In the theatre, actors say this to one another to bring good luck.*
5	*When you have narrowly avoided misfortune.*
4	*When someone fails a test or exam.*
2	*When someone wins at a game, and has never played the game before.*

EXERCISE 4

Ways of predicting the future

Match the method with its definition:

| 1 Palmistry | 2 Astrology | 3 Graphology | 4 Tarot |

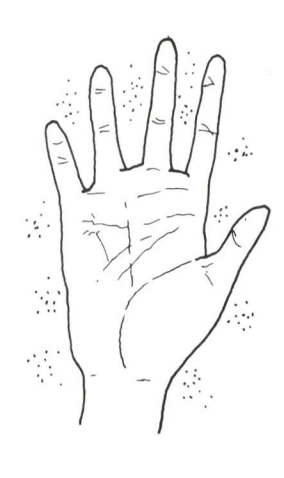

[3] The study of handwriting which claims to be able to reveal secrets about the person's life and/or personality.

[2] Predicting the future by studying the movements of the stars and planets.

[4] Revealing secrets about an individual's past, present and future by means of a set of special cards.

[1] Using the lines on the palm of the hand to predict future events.

EXERCISE 5

Match the following to make expressions connected with prediction:

1 to wish   [2] in fate
2 to believe   [4] tea leaves
3 to predict   [5] a crystal ball
4 to read   [3] the future
5 to gaze into   [1] someone good luck

EXERCISE 6

Now match the following with their opposites:

1 good luck   [4] logic
2 belief   [1] misfortune
3 lucky   [2] disbelief
4 superstition   [3] unlucky

18

EXERCISE 7

Fill the gaps in the following sentences with the correct word:

| fortune | chance | bargain | opportunity | luck |

1 By ____chance____ , I had my camera with me at the time of the accident.

2 I hope I have the ____opportunity____ to meet your parents over the weekend.

3 They say you'll have bad ____luck____ for seven years if you break a mirror.

4 He worked hard at his career and fame and ____fortune____ seemed to follow him wherever he went.

5 At these low prices, everything's a ____bargain____ .

EXERCISE 8

QUIZ - How superstitious are you?

Do this simple quiz to find out whether you depend on logic or superstition to get you through life!

1 Do you ever have your coffee grounds or tea-leaves read?
   ☐ never   ☐ sometimes   ☐ often

2 Do you read your horoscope?
   ☐ never   ☐ sometimes   ☐ often

3 Do you have a `lucky charm', i.e. something you carry around with you or wear to bring you good luck?
   ☐ yes   ☐ no

4 Do you ever wish others `Good Luck'?
   ☐ never   ☐ sometimes   ☐ often

5 Do you have, or do you believe you have, a lucky number?
   ☐ yes   ☐ no

When you have answered the questions, add up your score, using this simple points system:

never	no	sometimes	often	yes
0	0	2	3	3

Conclusions

0- 5 : You are a true sceptic! Your feet are firmly on the ground and you don't wait for luck to come to you; you go out and get it for yourself!

6-11 : You are quite superstitious, but you have a logical head on your shoulders.

12-15 : You are extremely superstitious. Look out for those ladders!

animals

EXERCISE 1

Some animals can be trained to work for us; dogs are an example.

Can you match the type of dog below with the job it commonly carries out?

1 guide dog   **3** rounding up sheep on a farm

2 guard dog   **4** sniffing out bombs or chemicals, tracking suspected criminals using scent

3 sheep dog   **1** helping to lead the blind

4 police dog   **2** protecting a house or its owners from danger of intruders

EXERCISE 2

Sort the following into the correct groups:

ant   goose   fly   clam   mussel   mosquito   duck   crab   pigeon   cockroach   turkey   lobster   cricket   ostrich   shrimp

INSECTS	BIRDS	SEA CREATURES
ant	goose	clam
fly	duck	mussel
mosquito	pigeon	crab
cockroach	turkey	lobster
cricket	ostrich	shrimp

Unit 5 Animals

EXERCISE 3

Match the collective noun with the correct animal group:

| elephants | hounds | fish | bees | sheep |

1 a flock of   sheep
2 a pack of   hounds
3 a shoal of   fish
4 a herd of   elephants
5 a swarm of   bees

EXERCISE 4

Human bodies are covered with **skin** and **hair**. Match these animals with the correct skin covering:

1 bear
2 horse
3 fish
4 tortoise
5 bird

5 feathers
4 shell
1 fur
2 hair
3 scales

EXERCISE 5

Some animals are associated with certain countries or places. Solve the anagrams below using the clues provided:

L A M C E   CAMEL

➥ a desert animal with one or two humps on its back

21

OKORNAAG — **KANGAROO**
➤ an Australian animal which moves by jumping

PAROL BRAE — **POLAR BEAR**
➤ a white bear living in north polar regions

AMPPITOOHPSU — **HIPPOPOTAMUS**
➤ a large African river animal with short legs and thick dark skin

AREBZ — **ZEBRA**
➤ an African wild animal with a striped body

EXERCISE 6

Read the text and fill the gaps with the correct word in the right form:

| dog | animal | wolf | mouse | horse |

Animals appear in many stories for children. Sometimes the animal represents fear or evil, like the big, bad __wolf__ in the story of Little Red Riding Hood. In such stories, there is invariably a 'happy ending' involving the death of the wolf and a victory of Good over Evil. In other stories, animals are friendly towards humans, like the __dog__ Lassie and in the tales of 'The Lone Ranger' where the __horse__, Silver, is shown to have the qualities of loyalty and affection. In the Fables of Aesop, __animals__ are given human characteristics, and the stories are used to expose human failings or weaknesses; we are meant to learn a lesson from them. Of course, animals have always appeared in cartoons to provide humour, the most famous being Mickey __mouse__, Bugs Bunny, and Tom and Jerry.

EXERCISE 7

Complete the following by deciding which animal is involved:

wolf	rabbit	horse	wolf	pigs

1. A famous fable by Aesop is `The boy who cried __wolf__ ?

2. A __wolf__ wanted to eat Little Red Riding Hood.

3. In one famous fairy tale, three little __pigs__ each tried to build themselves a house.

4. The Lone Ranger trusted his faithful __horse__, Silver.

5. Bugs Bunny is a cartoon __rabbit__.

EXERCISE 8

Animals

☞ We sometimes attribute certain 'human' qualities to animals; for example, we often describe dogs as being 'faithful' and a pig as being 'greedy'.

Which special qualities do you associate with the following animals? Read the sentences and decide which animal is being described.

owl	cat	dog	lion	fox	elephant

1. It is sly and cunning. __fox__

2. It is said to be wise. __owl__

3. It is king of the jungle. __lion__

4. It has nine lives. __cat__

5. It never forgets. __elephant__

6. It is man's best friend. __dog__

23

socialising

> To most people in Western society, socialising is an important concept. The purposes of getting together with other people are varied: usually the main reason for social activities is relaxation or enjoyment, for example friends meeting on a Saturday night for a drink. Sometimes the gathering has a more formal or celebratory function (e.g. a wedding), or you can go out for a meal and mix business with pleasure by entertaining a prospective client, and so on.

EXERCISE 1

Below are five different social functions. Unscramble the letters to find out what they are (they all involve food).

D D N I W G E — **WEDDING**
➥ marriage is involved

E I N D N R T Y A P R — **DINNER PARTY**
➥ an evening meal for a group of people

C I P I C N — **PICNIC**
➥ an outdoor meal

C A R B E U B E — **BARBECUE**
➥ a meal which consists of food cooked outside on a grill

S A F T E — **FEAST**
➥ a large quantity of food, wine, etc. usually accompanied by celebrations

EXERCISE 2

*Eating out or with company sometimes means we have to respect certain conventions of **politeness** or **etiquette**. Put in the correct verb to complete the list of table manners below:*

| cut | suck | slurp | lick | close | chew | speak | keep |

1. __Keep__ your elbows off the table.
2. __Close__ your mouth when chewing your food.
3. Don't __speak__ with your mouth full.
4. Don't __lick__ your fingers.
5. __Chew__ your food slowly.
6. Don't __suck__ loudly through a straw.
7. __Cut__ your food into small pieces.
8. Don't __slurp__ drinks or soup loudly.

EXERCISE 3

Put in order of importance the following reasons for socialising:

- [ ] to enjoy yourself
- [ ] to forget your problems
- [ ] to meet people
- [ ] to dance
- [ ] to celebrate a special occasion
- [ ] to see your friends
- [ ] to find out the latest gossip
- [ ] to get out of the house

EXERCISE 4

Tick the following if you have ever been there. Put an **L** next to the ones you have not been to but would like to attend or visit and an **X** next to the ones that definitely do not interest you:

✓ – L – X		✓ – L – X	
	ballet		art gallery
	opera		zoo
	theatre		restaurant
	concert (pop/rock)		disco
	concert (classical)		carnival
	museum		wedding

Can you give reasons for your preferences?

Example Answer: Students should write their own.

I would like to attend a wedding because weddings are very happy occasions.

EXERCISE 5

Fill the gaps in the sentences with the correct word from the box below:

chat argue whisper gossip shout mumble

1 I'd like to have a ___chat___ with you about your holiday plans.

2 There's no need to ___shout___; I can hear you quite well.

3 Why do you have to ___argue___ with me every time I make a suggestion?

4 Don't waste my time with this idle ___gossip___.

5 Speak up! I can't understand what you're saying when you ___mumble___ like that.

6 ___Whisper___ in my ear so nobody else can hear.

EXERCISE 6

Words connected with humour

Match the following:

1. to tell
2. to make fun of
3. to pull

[3] someone's leg
[1] a joke
[2] someone

Fill the gaps with the correct phrase:

1. Everyone expects the best man to __tell__ a few __jokes__ at a wedding.

2. You shouldn't __make fun of someone__ just because they make a mistake.

3. Don't believe Uncle Jake's stories about being a spy; he's just __pulling your leg__.

EXERCISE 7

Use the following words to complete the sentences which follow:

| kidding | silly | witty | hilarious | funny | amusing |

1. You might find it __amusing__ to write slogans on the school walls, but I certainly don't!

2. "I've just seen George Michael in the supermarket!" "No __kidding__!"

3. You look a bit __funny__ in that dress; maybe it's too big for you.

4. Don't be __silly__, dear. Of course I don't believe in UFOs.

5. He has a great sense of humour and a very __witty__ turn of phrase.

6. Did you see The Benny Hill Show last night? It was absolutely __hilarious__.

celebrations

EXERCISE 1

Celebrations and culture

How do you celebrate your birthday?

> Example Answer:
> Students should write their own.

<u>I have a big party and invite all my school friends.</u>

What traditional customs (e.g. music, food, etc.) surround these events?

<u>We usually have a big cake with candles. I have to blow out the candles and make a wish. If I can blow them all out in one go, it is said that my wish will come true!</u>

EXERCISE 2

Religious festivals

Each of the following Christian festivals has a special name; match the festival with its name from the list given below:

| 1 Good Friday | 2 Ash Wednesday | 3 Christmas | 4 Easter | 5 Epiphany |

- [4] The resurrection of Christ
- [3] The birth of Christ
- [2] The beginning of Lent (fasting)
- [5] The visit of the three wise men to the baby Jesus
- [1] The death of Christ

EXERCISE 3

The following are all non-religious festivals. Can you match each with the date on which it falls?

| (a) 31st October | (b) 1st April | (c) 14th February | (d) 4th July |
| (e) 1st May | (f) 5th November |

- [f] Guy Fawkes' Night
- [c] St Valentine's Day
- [d] American Independence Day
- [a] Hallowe'en
- [e] Labour Day
- [b] April Fools' Day

EXERCISE 4

Three Celebrations

Complete each paragraph using the words in the boxes:

| sender | lovers | identity | cards | traditionally |

St Valentine's Day is a day when **lovers** celebrate by sending each other **cards** and flowers. Great mystery is supposed to surround the **sender** of the card who **traditionally** does not reveal his or her **identity**.

| sightings | tricks | visitors | victims | growing |

On the first of April each year, hundreds of **tricks**, old and new, are played on unwary **victims**. Memorable tricks of the past have included a television news report claiming that spaghetti was **growing** in the fields of Italy and claims of various **sightings** of 'little green men', supposedly **visitors** from the planet Mars. All stunts have to be completed by 12:00 midday, however, or they cease to be valid.

| traditional | apples | house | celebrate | dress |

Hallowe'en is the night when witches and evil spirits are banished. People often **celebrate** with fancy **dress** parties, dressing in **traditional** style as witches and ghosts. Games sometimes played include 'Trick or Treat', where children go from **house** to house hoping to fill an empty bag with sweets and toys.

A game called 'apple bobbing' is also played: **apples** are placed in a bowl of water and everyone has to try to catch one using their mouths only – no hands! Of course, everyone gets very wet!

29

EXERCISE 5

Match the following to form phrases:

1	to wish	5	someone a card
2	to welcome	3	a special occasion
3	to celebrate	2	someone to a new place
4	to greet	4	your guests at a party
5	to send	1	someone a Happy Birthday

EXERCISE 6

NOUN	ADJECTIVE
religion	religious
culture	**cultural**
tradition	traditional
custom	**customary**

Complete the above and then fill the gaps in the sentences below:

1 It's _____**traditional**_____ in many countries to have a Carnival every year as a celebration.

2 In Japan, it's _____**customary**_____ to take off your shoes before entering a house.

3 The _____**religious**_____ beliefs of some societies prohibit the consumption of pork.

4 _____**Cultural**_____ differences can lead to misunderstandings: in some countries drinking alcohol is encouraged as a social activity while in others it is strictly forbidden.

EXERCISE 7

Cultural knowledge quiz

Match the following:

1	Pharaohs	2	The former Royal Family of Russia
2	Tsars	3	One of two traditionally opposing African tribes
3	Zulus	1	The kings of Ancient Egypt
4	Emperors	5	The original inhabitants of Australia
5	Aborigines	4	The leaders of the Roman Empire

Where would you see the following famous sights?

1	The Eiffel Tower	2	New York
2	The Statue of Liberty	4	Athens
3	Big Ben	1	Paris
4	The Acropolis	6	Sydney
5	The Great Wall	3	London
6	The Opera House	5	China

Which forms of headgear do you associate with the following countries?

1	stetson	4	Mexico
2	beret	6	England
3	fez	1	U.S.A.
4	sombrero	5	Pakistan
5	turban	2	France
6	bowler	3	Morocco

31

clothes

EXERCISE 1

Which of the following materials are synthetic (man-made) and which are made from natural fibres?

synthetic	natural	MATERIAL
	✔	cotton
✔		nylon
	✔	wool
	✔	silk
	✔	leather
	✔	fur
✔		plastic

EXERCISE 2

Choose from the following to complete the sentences below:

fashion   fashionable   out of fashion   out-dated   old-fashioned

1 Flared trousers and flowery shirts were ___fashionable___ in the 1960s and 1970s.

2 Magazines like 'Vogue' provide ideas and information about what's in ___fashion___ at the moment.

3 I was delighted when I came across a(n) ___old-fashioned___ spinning wheel in the antique shop.

4 Platform shoes have been ___out of fashion___ for a long time but I think they're going to make a comeback.

5 Food shortages in Russian shops are due in part to the primitive tools and ___out-dated___ farming methods used in the agriculture industry there.

EXERCISE 3

Below are three words which describe the way people are dressed. Read the definitions and then complete the sentences which follow.

☞ **smart** — well-dressed; neat
trendy — very modern; of the latest fashion
casual — informal and comfortable

1 When I'm not working, I like to wear __casual__ clothes around the house.

2 The first time I saw him was at a disco; I remember I was wearing a __trendy__ mini-dress from my favourite boutique.

3 I'm going to buy a __smart__ new suit to wear to the office

EXERCISE 4

Look at the pictures of different styles of knitwear and label them correctly with the following:

1 cardigan   2 polo-neck   3 V-neck   4 crew-neck   5 turtle-neck

EXERCISE 5

Look at the five items of clothing and choose the most suitable to complete the following sentences:

floral dress   baggy trousers   knitted pullover   fitted jacket   pleated skirt

1. She's got a __floral dress__ she likes to wear in the summer.

2. The old man was wearing __baggy trousers__ held up with a brown leather belt.

3. That __pleated skirt__ reminds me of my school uniform!

4. My Mum gave me a hand-__knitted pullover__ for Christmas.

5. I bought a __fitted jacket__ and skirt to wear to the job interview.

EXERCISE 6

Look at the pictures and label the following types of tie:

1 bow tie   2 neck tie   3 cravat

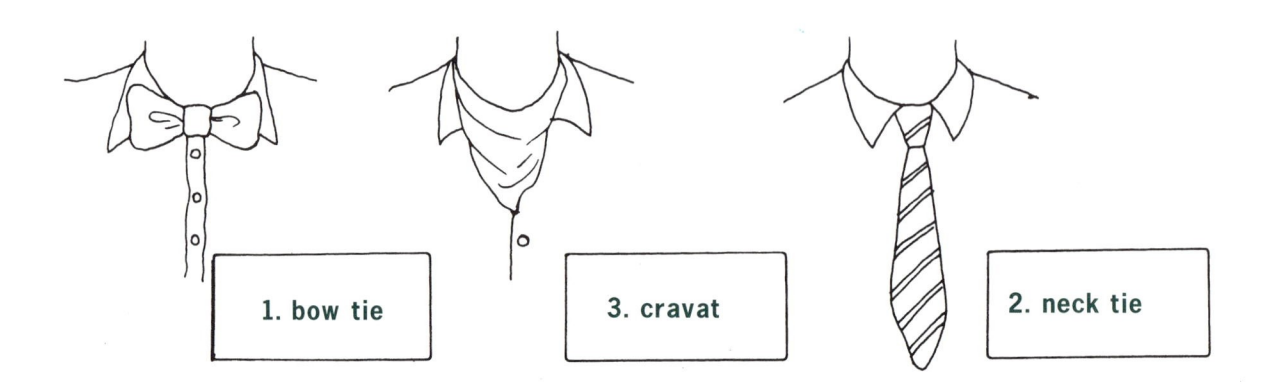

1. bow tie

3. cravat

2. neck tie

EXERCISE 7

Complete the sentences with the words from the box in their right forms:

| button | zip | elastic | lace | belt |

1 My four-year-old son has already learnt to do up the ____laces____ on his shoes.

2 The ____zip____ on my anorak got stuck and I couldn't undo it.

3 One of the ____buttons____ has fallen off my shirt; could you sew it on for me?

4 It's time I bought some new underwear — everything I've got is so old the ____elastic____ has gone.

5 If I didn't wear a ____belt____ with these trousers, they would probably fall down!

EXERCISE 8

With which places do you associate these items of clothing?

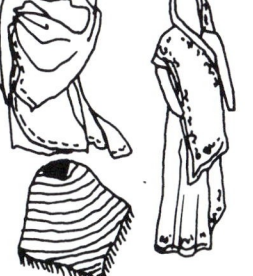

1 kilt   [2] Ancient Rome
2 toga   [5] Mexico
3 sari   [1] Scotland
4 kimono   [3] India
5 poncho   [4] Japan

EXERCISE 9

Match the items of headgear below with their owners:

1 bowler hat   [3] builder
2 wig   [5] nun
3 hard hat   [4] fireman
4 helmet   [2] judge
5 veil   [1] businessman

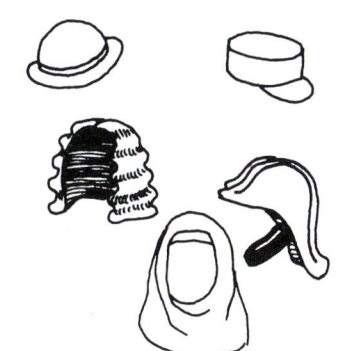

family & marriage

EXERCISE 1

☞ If you fill in an official form, such as a census, you may be asked to categorise your marital status into one of the following groups:
- single
- divorced
- separated
- married
- widowed
- engaged

Make sure you know what all these words mean.

EXERCISE 2

Match the males with the females in the following categories:

1. mother-in-law
2. spinster
3. widow
4. fiancée
5. ex-wife

[4] fiancé
[3] widower
[1] father-in-law
[5] ex-husband
[2] bachelor

EXERCISE 3

Now complete these sentences to define the words given below:

| spinster   widower   engaged   ex-wife   fiancé |

1. A man whose wife has died is a __widower__.

2. A woman who has never married is a __spinster__.

3. A man who is engaged to be married is somebody's __fiance__.

4. A woman who has divorced her husband becomes his __ex-wife__.

5. Before they get married, a couple usually gets __engaged__.

EXERCISE 4

Marriage

Fill the gaps in the text with the following words:

| weds married marriage wedding |

Tom and Laura's ___wedding___ took place on a beautiful day in June. The priest who ___married___ them was an old friend of the family and made them feel very relaxed. After the ceremony, they all went to sign the ___marriage___ certificate and the newly-___weds___ joined their family and friends for the reception.

EXERCISE 5

☞ Do you know the difference between the terms 'marriage' and 'wedding'?
marriage - the legal union of husband and wife
wedding - the ceremony and all the festivities connected with marriage

Fill the gaps to complete the following sentences. Use **marriage** or **wedding**:

1 Do you believe in ___marriage___ ?

2 I've been invited to Paul and Sarah's ___wedding___ .

3 Their ___marriage___ lasted 22 years.

4 I went to their ___wedding___ but the rest of the family didn't approve of their ___marriage___ .

EXERCISE 6

Below is a text describing a typical English wedding. Rearrange the letters given in bold type to complete the paragraph. Then put them in the grid below:

A wedding in England is a very special occasion which requires months of preparation. Traditionally, the ❶ **RBEDI** wears a long white dress and ❷ **ELVI** , the ❸ **OGROM** wears a suit and all the guests dress up smartly. The bride may be attended by ❹ **DIABREMISDS** and/or pageboys while the ❺ **ETSB NAM** stands beside the groom.

Special religious songs called ❻ **YHSMN** are sung in church and after the ❼ **MERCENYO** is over, the newly-weds leave the church together and their friends and relatives throw ❽ **NOFITCET** over them. Later, everyone enjoys themselves at the reception, where they eat a wedding breakfast and toast the ❾ **UPOLCE** before they leave for their ❿ **NYONOEHMO** .

37

1	bride	6	hymns
2	veil	7	ceremony
3	groom	8	confetti
4	bridesmaids	9	couple
5	best man	10	honeymoon

Look at the sketch below and label the following:

bride   groom   bouquet   veil   ring   best man   bridesmaid   priest

EXERCISE 7

Here are some verb phrases connected with family, marriage and relationships:

going out with   am close to   keep in touch with   left on the shelf

Use them to fill the gaps in the following sentences:

1 My sister's been __going out with__ her boyfriend for over two years but I don't think they'll get married.

2 I __am close to__ my parents even though I don't live at home any more.

3 I still __keep in touch with__ my French pen-friend and I hope one day she'll come and visit me.

4 She's thirty-five, still single and starting to feel as though she's been __left on the shelf__.

EXERCISE 8

Affixes

Choose from the prefixes below to complete the following sentences:

| un- | ex- | re- | be- |

1 I'll _____**re**_name_ my children after I get divorced.

2 My _____**ex**_-husband's_ family don't speak to me any more.

3 She became another _____**un**_married_ mother living in the city.

4 He's been very _____**un**_happy_ since the divorce.

5 I tried to _____**be**_friend_ her but she preferred to be on her own.

EXERCISE 9

Check your understanding of the vocabulary in this unit by answering the following questions:

1 What is your present marital status? **single/married/engaged**.

2 A man who has never been married is called a **bachelor**.

3 **Confetti** is often thrown at the couple during the wedding.

4 The bride throws her **bouquet** of flowers over her shoulder after the wedding.

5 People who are members of the same family are called relations or **relatives**.

letters

> Letter-writing is bound by certain conventions, as are all forms of communication, written or spoken.

EXERCISE 1

Find out what the following abbreviations stand for. The answers will be provided at the end of the unit.

ABBREVIATIONS	
i.e.	i.e. — id est (that is)
P.S.	P.S. — postscript
w.p.m.	w.p.m. words per minute
R.S.V.P.	R.S.V.P. — respondez s'il vous plait (please reply)
a.s.a.p.	a.s.a.p. — as soon as possible
C.O.D.	C.O.D. — cash on delivery
C.V.	C.V. — curriculum vitae
etc.	Etc. — et cetera (and the rest ; and so on)

EXERCISE 2

If you can, look at the keyboard of a typewriter or a computer and find and write down the following punctuation items:

.	full stop	!	exclamation mark
,	comma	?	question mark
A	capital `a'	:	colon
_	dash	;	semi-colon
( )	brackets	'	apostrophe
" "	quotation marks	*	asterisk

40

EXERCISE 3

Sentences are the basic units of written language. They are made up of words and put together to form paragraphs. Put the following units of language into order of 'size':

PARAGRAPH
SENTENCE
PHRASE
WORD
SYLLABLE
LETTER

PARAGRAPH

PHRASE

SENTENCE

SYLLABLE

LETTER (OF THE ALPHABET)

WORD

EXERCISE 4

Match the following words into pairs which have similar meanings:

1 note

2 write

3 writer

4 brochure

3	author
4	pamphlet
1	memo
2	jot down

EXERCISE 5

Office jargon

Match the following with their respective meanings:

1 A note circulated in an office between certain individuals

2 A piece of computer hardware which stores information

3 Pens, paper clips and other office equipment

4 A piece of paper with official information on it

5 A place where papers etc. are kept for reference purposes, often in alphabetical order

4	document
1	memo (memorandum)
5	file
2	disk
3	stationery

41

EXERCISE 6

Use the words provided below to complete the text of this business letter:

| candidate | position | referees | application | recommended |
| temporary | qualifications | experience |

P.Trumper Esq.
Barsted Philharmonic Orchestra
Lamed Ave.
London W12

Mr D. Fiddle
36 Cold Corner Terrace
Beltup
London E16

Dear Mr Fiddle,

Thank you very much for your letter of __applications__ and C.V., which we read with great interest. Your __qualifications__ from the University of Dullshill and relevant __experience__ of working with composers made you a very strong __candidate__ and it is therefore with regret that I must inform you that we are unable at this time to offer you a permanent __position__ as concert violinist. However, I have __recommend__ you to the board and there is a possibility of a __temporary__ post becoming vacant in the near future. If you would provide the names and addresses of two __referees__, the board will contact you to let you know if you have been successful. The details of your letter will, of course, remain strictly confidential.

Yours sincerely,

P. Trumper

EXERCISE 7   Related vocabulary

Choose the word which best completes the following sentences:

| ordered | sent | received | registered | mail |

1 The office junior usually gets the job of making coffee and opening the ___mail___ .

2 If you have something valuable to send in a parcel, it's advisable to send it by ___registered___ post.

3 He ___sent___ off for the brochure three weeks ago but it still hasn't arrived.

4 Thank you for your letter which I ___received___ this morning.

5 The furniture which I ___ordered___ was damaged in transit and I would like a complete refund or a replacement.

EXERCISE 8

Use the abbreviations in the box to complete the following sentences:

1 Send an up-to-date copy of your ___C.V.___ along with your job application.

2 She's a fast typist; she can do over 90 ___w.p.m.___ .

3 The vacancy has been filled, ___i.e.___ the job no longer exists.

4 If you want to swim, bring your bathing costume, a towel, suncream ___etc.___ .

5 You pay a small deposit now and the rest is ___C.O.D.___ .

6 I'm sorry about the delay. Your order will be sent ___a.s.a.p.___ .

7 I'll write again soon. Love from Daniel.
___P.S.___ Did you see the match on Saturday?

8 You are invited to a party to celebrate the engagement of Peter and Sonya. ___R.S.V.P.___ by 11th April.

☞	**etc.**	*et cetera* (and the rest; and so on)
	i.e.	*id est* (that is)
	P.S.	postscript
	w.p.m.	words per minute
	a.s.a.p.	as soon as possible
	R.S.V.P.	*répondez s'il vous plaît* (please reply)
	C.O.D.	cash on delivery
	C.V.	*curriculum vitae*

travel

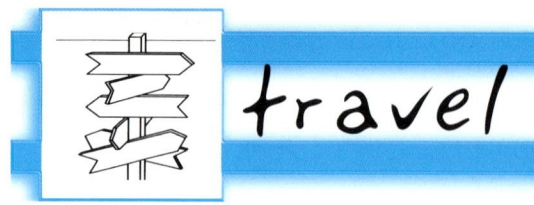

EXERCISE 1

Below are words connected with various means of transport. Can you sort them into the correct categories? (There are five in each category.)

track　lane　terminal　petrol　station　park　airport　garage　platform　check-in　mirror　crossing　runway　line　pilot

RAILWAY	PLANE	CAR
track	terminal	lane
station	airport	petrol
platform	check-in	park
crossing	runway	garage
line	pilot	mirror

EXERCISE 2

Select the correct word from those given to complete the sentences below:

1 There's a **delay/<u>diversion</u>**. We have to take a different route.

2 Let's take the **<u>motorway</u>/driveway** to avoid the traffic jams in town.

3 Some trains have been **dismissed/<u>cancelled</u>** because of staff shortage.

4 If you don't want to get into trouble with the police, keep within the **<u>speed</u>/driving** limit.

5 Motorways and dual carriageways have more than one traffic **road/<u>lane</u>**.

EXERCISE 3

Giving directions

Fill the gaps in the dialogue below using the following words:

| set | keep | reach | get | junction |

A : Excuse me, can you tell me how to get to the leisure centre, please?

B : Yes, of course. You __keep__ going until you __reach__ the first __junction__. Turn right and then take the first left after the railway crossing. Keep going until you __get__ to the second __set__ of traffic lights. The leisure centre is on your right.

A : Thank you.

EXERCISE 4

☞ What should this word read?

AMBULANCE

Why is it sometimes written like this?
It is written backwards so it can be read in car mirrors.

The ambulance service is part of the **emergency services**. What other emergency services exist?
The Police Force, The Fire Brigade, Search and Rescue, The Coast Guard etc.

EXERCISE 5

Fill the gaps in the text below to complete the paragraph:

| vehicles | priority | pavements | emergency | way |

Police cars, fire engines and ambulances have special __priority__ on the road. In an __emergency__, they do not have to stop at traffic lights, can mount __pavements__ to avoid obstacles in their way and other drivers must keep to the left in order to leave space for these __vehicles__ to pass. The noise of the siren tells other road users to make __way__.

EXERCISE 6

Man-made systems

Match the following well-known engineering feats with the correct description:

1 The Channel Tunnel

2 The Menai Bridge

3 The Grand Canal

4 The M1

5 Spaghetti Junction

2	It joins the mainland of Wales to the island of Anglesea.
3	This provides a transport system for the inhabitants of Venice.
4	This is the name of an important motorway in Britain.
1	An ambitious project which aimed to provide an undersea link between England and France.
5	The name given to a place in the Midlands where a number of important roads meet.

EXERCISE 7

There are a number of different names for the places where we walk or drive. Below are some. Choose the correct phrase to complete the expressions appropriately:

| alley | avenue | lane | street | road |

1 a tree-lined _____avenue_____

2 a country _____lane_____

3 Oxford _____Road/Street_____

4 a back _____alley_____

5 a one-way _____street/road_____

EXERCISE 8

Label the cars correctly using the words given in the box:

| boot | bumper | bonnet | headlight | number-plate | tyre | roof-rack |

Labels on cars: boot, roof-rack, headlight, bonnet, number-plate, bumper, tyre

EXERCISE 9

Match the following vehicles or vessels with the correct sketches:

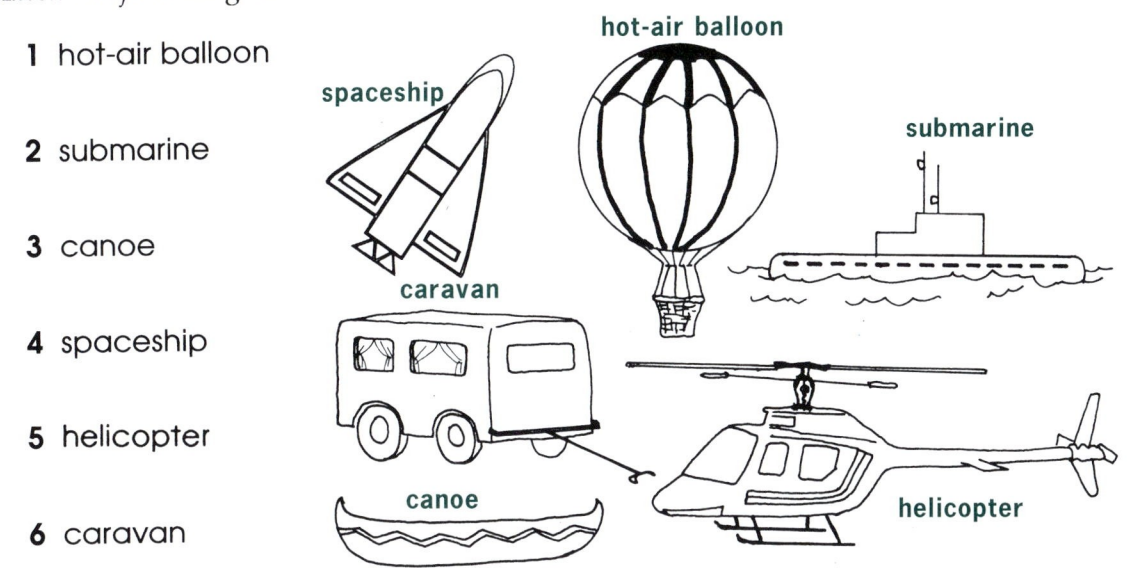

1 hot-air balloon

2 submarine

3 canoe

4 spaceship

5 helicopter

6 caravan

Sketches labelled: spaceship, hot-air balloon, submarine, caravan, canoe, helicopter

Now use this vocabulary to do the exercise below:

1 You paddle this down a river. — canoe

2 A kind of house on wheels. — caravan

3 An underwater naval vessel. — submarine

4 This is not an aeroplane but it can take you high up into the clouds. — hot-air balloon

5 We crossed the sea by this instead of by boat. — helicopter

6 A vehicle for travelling to the moon or to other planets. — spaceship

cookery

EXERCISE 1
Ethnic dishes

From which countries do these traditional dishes originate?

| Mexico | Italy | England | Spain | Greece | Japan |
| India | Germany | France | China | | |

DISHES	COUNTRY	DISHES	COUNTRY
Paella	Spain	Fish and chips	England
Sauerkraut	Germany	Snails in garlic	France
Moussaka	Greece	Spaghetti	Italy
Fried rice	China	Chilli	Mexico
Sushi	Japan	Curry	India

EXERCISE 2
Imports and exports

Match the country with a product it is famous for:

1 New Zealand

2 Holland

3 Denmark

4 France

5 Greece

2	cheese
4	wine
1	lamb
5	olives
3	bacon

48

EXERCISE 3

Sort the following into SEAFOOD and MEAT categories:

squid   veal   tongue   prawns   mussels
chops   liver   lobster   tuna   steak

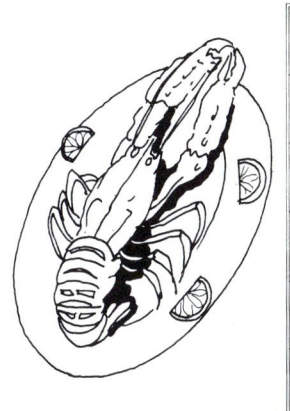

SEAFOOD	MEAT
squid	veal
prawns	tongue
mussels	chops
lobster	liver
tuna	steak

EXERCISE 4

Ways of cooking

Match the following to make common expressions connected with cooking:

1 bake

2 roast

3 fry

4 smoke(d)

5 boil

[3] an egg

[5] some spaghetti

[1] a cake

[2] a chicken

[4] salmon

EXERCISE 5

Find five different ways of cooking in the following anagrams:

L I G R L E D	GRILLED
E B I O D L	BOILED
K D A B E	BAKED
R F E D I	FRIED
W E S T D E	STEWED

EXERCISE 6

What do these words have in common?

> cut   carve   chop   slice   peel   grate

All are verbs connected with the use of knife-like or sharp objects.

Use a dictionary to find out when each word is used. Then complete the recipe for a Spanish omelette below with correct forms of five of these words:

To make a Spanish omelette, first __chop/slice__ the onions and fry them gently in a little oil. Next, __peel__ the potatoes and __cut__ them up into cubes. Fry these until they begin to soften and then add some finely __chopped__ seasonal vegetables: carrots and peas are popular choices. Beat the eggs with some milk, salt and pepper and put them into the pan, on top of the vegetables. Leave to allow the eggs to cook thoroughly underneath and sprinkle with __grated__ cheese before browning under the grill for a few minutes.

EXERCISE 7

Fill the gaps in the sentences below with words from the box below:

> sliced   carved   grilled   stuffed   peeled

1 A popular Greek hors d'oeuvre is __stuffed__ vine leaves.

2 Oranges need to be __peeled__ before you eat them.

3 Bread is __sliced__ and buttered to make sandwiches.

4 Grandfather __carved__ the joint and we all enjoyed the rich flavour of the meat.

5 Sausages lose some of their fat when they are __grilled__.

50

EXERCISE 8

Quick Food-and-Drink Quiz

With which countries do you associate the following drinks?

1 ouzo
2 whisky
3 coffee
4 beer
5 vodka
6 tea
7 rum
8 sangria

[4] Germany
[3] Brazil
[6] China
[7] Jamaica
[1] Greece
[2] Scotland
[8] Spain
[5] Russia

EXERCISE 9

Answer the following questions:

1 Which vegetable did Popeye eat to make him strong?

spinach

2 What was the forbidden fruit in the Garden of Eden?

the apple

3 Which food is produced by bees?

honey

4 From which fruit is the drink *cider* made?

apple

5 Tagliatelli, tortellini and rigatoni are all types of pasta; from which country does pasta originate?

Italy

people

EXERCISE 1   Appearance

> You may have heard a number of different words used to express 'fat' or 'thin' when describing people. Here are some examples:
>
> **chubby   plump   overweight**
>
> all mean '**fat**' in some way, while
>
> **slim   skinny   frail**
>
> are ways of saying '**thin**'.
>
> The reasons for the variety of expressions is that each word contains more in its meaning than just **fat** or **thin**. We use **chubby** or **plump** in an affectionate way, often to describe children. It can also be applied to other people and is more polite than the word **fat**. **Overweight** is also a more polite expression than **fat** and is sometimes used in a clinical way, by doctors or officials.
> **Slim** is a complimentary word for thinness, while **skinny** is slightly derogatory and suggests **too thin**.
> **Frail** is used most often for old people and denotes weakness as well as thinness.

Complete these sentences with the correct word:

1. What do you say to someone when you don't want to hurt their feelings but you are concerned that they are putting on a lot of weight?
   Aren't you a little ___overweight___ ?

2. What might you say to a child who is gaining weight?
   You're getting quite ___plump___, aren't you!

3. What could you say about a fashion model's enviable figure?
   She's very ___slim___ with long legs.

4. She's eighty-two years old, small and very ___frail___.

5. You should eat more; you're getting very ___skinny/thin___.

6. He's a sweet baby, with ___chubby___ pink cheeks.

EXERCISE 2

Find the villains — police offer reward!

Police report file number: 253

At approximately 22:20 hours on the night of 22nd September, two people were seen getting out of an X-registered Ford Escort in Brixton High Street. They then forced entry to Jones' Jeweller's shop, and made off with valuables worth over £250,000. The alarm was raised by a passer-by, who told the police that the thieves were dressed all in black: one was a woman aged 30-35, with short, spiky hair, thick lips and dangly ear-rings. The other was described as male, 35-40 years of age, bald, with thick eyebrows.

Can you pick out the suspects from the line-up below? [see pictures]

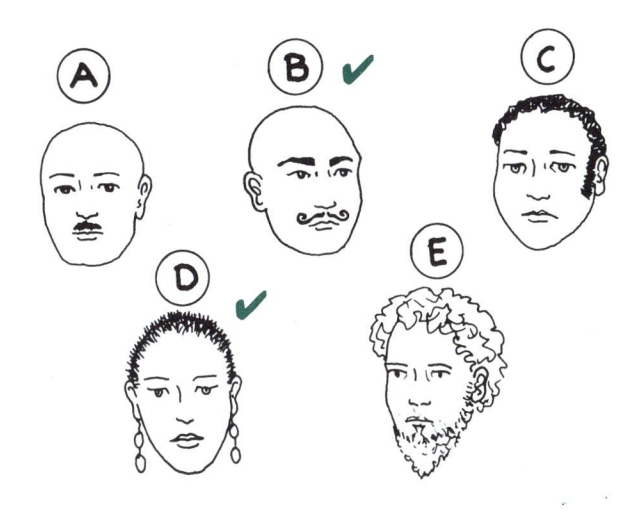

B ✔
D ✔

EXERCISE 3

Character

Match the opposites in the following list of character traits:

1	sensitive		3	miserable
2	clumsy		9	tactless
3	cheerful		5	unreliable
4	loyal		2	graceful
5	reliable		8	unsympathetic
6	trustworthy		1	insensitive
7	tolerant		4	disloyal
8	sympathetic		6	untrustworthy
9	tactful		7	intolerant

EXERCISE 4

To show that you can understand and use the words in EXERCISE 3 correctly, select the correct word to fill the gaps in the sentences below:

1 I have just heard from a ___reliable___ source that this isn't the first time such an accident has occurred.

2 I have complete faith in her; she has always been a very ___loyal/trustworthy___ employee.

3 You should be more ___tolerant___ towards people who have different opinions from yours.

4 He's a very ___sensitive___ child; he gets upset easily if the others tease him.

5 She's so ___clumsy___ when she's not wearing her glasses; she trips over everything.

EXERCISE 5

From the sentences below, decide which of the three words given is the correct one:

1 Someone who is happy one day and miserable the next is **stubborn/moody/intolerant**.

2 If you've just passed an exam, you feel very **pleased/contented/cheerful** with yourself.

3 If you don't say `please' and `thank you', then you're not being very **kind/polite/nice**.

4 Once you decide something, nothing will change your mind; you're very **stable/constant/stubborn**.

5 If you accept other people's points of view, you are **sympathetic/tolerant/tactful**.

6 You don't think before you speak; the moment you open your mouth, you say something **tactless/clumsy/rough**.

7 If you're always tripping over or breaking things, you are **clumsy/reckless/insensitive**.

8 If you always arrive at meetings at the correct time, you are **timely/punctual/loyal**.

EXERCISE 6

Divide the following characteristics into 'positive' or desirable characteristics and 'negative' ones:

> intelligent   disloyal   tolerant   reliable   stubborn   tactless   clumsy
> punctual   moody   patient   trustworthy   unsympathetic

POSITIVE	NEGATIVE
intelligent	disloyal
tolerant	stubborn
reliable	tactless
punctual	clumsy
patient	moody
trustworthy	unsympathetic

EXERCISE 7

Now write some sentences about yourself, including your positive and negative characteristics. Use some of the words above, as in the example:
e.g. *I'm a loyal friend. I don't say things behind my friends' backs.*

Example Only: I am reliable; people can depend on me to get things done.

I am punctual; I always arrive on time for my appointments.

I am moody; sometimes I get very angry with people over silly things, other times I am carefree.

the sea

EXERCISE 1

Look at the map below and insert the names of the five seas in the correct places:

> the Atlantic Ocean   the North Sea   the Mediterranean Sea
> the Caspian Sea   the Black Sea

- North Sea
- Black Sea
- Atlantic Ocean
- Caspian Sea
- Mediterranean Sea

EXERCISE 2

Match the sketches with the six popular watersports named below:

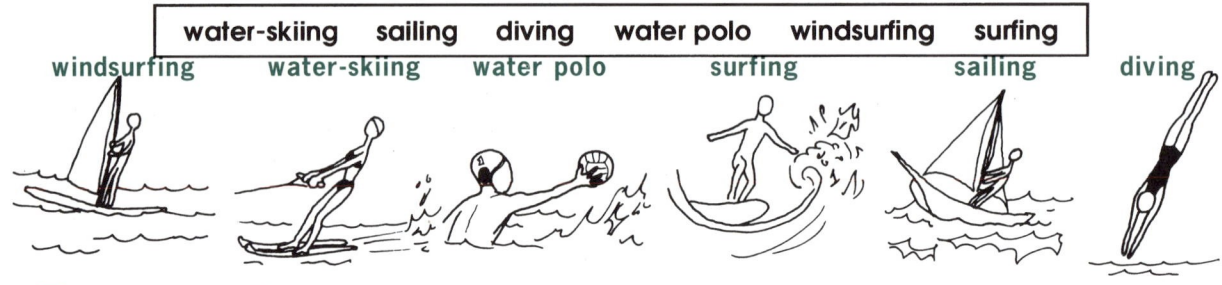

> water-skiing   sailing   diving   water polo   windsurfing   surfing

windsurfing   water-skiing   water polo   surfing   sailing   diving

EXERCISE 3

Find 8 types of water vessel in the anagrams below:

H I S P ➡ Our luggage was sent over by ____ship____.

A O B T ➡ They were rescued and brought to shore in a fishing ____boat____.

U G T ➡ A ____tug____ towed the ship into harbour.

C Y A H T ➡ We love sailing so much we're saving up to buy our own ____yacht____.

R F Y E R → If you go by cross-Channel ___ferry___, you can take your car with you.

N A C O E → The Indians travelled up river by ___canoe___.

D O O G N A L → We cruised the canals of Venice in a ___gondola___.

M B R U A N I S E → A ___submarine___ is often used in war because it can travel on the surface of the sea as well as below it.

EXERCISE 4

Use the words in the box below to form compound nouns with the word 'sea'; then use these compounds in the right form to complete the sentences below:

| horse | front | food | gull | bed | lion | side | sick | weed | shell |

1 The *sea* ___bed___ is the floor of the sea.

2 We ate fresh lobster, crabs, oysters and other *sea* ___food___ in a restaurant on the coast.

3 A small fish which resembles a very different animal is a *sea-* ___horse___.

4 A *sea-* ___lion___ is a large seal of the North Pacific Ocean.

5 I like to collect different kinds of *sea* ___shells___ when I go walking on the beach.

6 I'm not used to travelling by boat; I feel a little *sea* ___sick___.

7 *Sea* ___weed___ is a kind of plant which grows in the sea; a delicacy in some countries — the Japanese eat it fried.

8 I wanted a view of the sea so I booked into a hotel on the *sea* ___front___.

9 The *sea* ___side___ town of Folkestone is a popular summer holiday resort.

10 A flock of hungry *sea* ___gulls___ followed the ship for miles.

57

EXERCISE 5

Make sure you know the meaning of the words in the box below:

| flag | sail | mast | deck | steering wheel |

Now use them to complete the diagram:

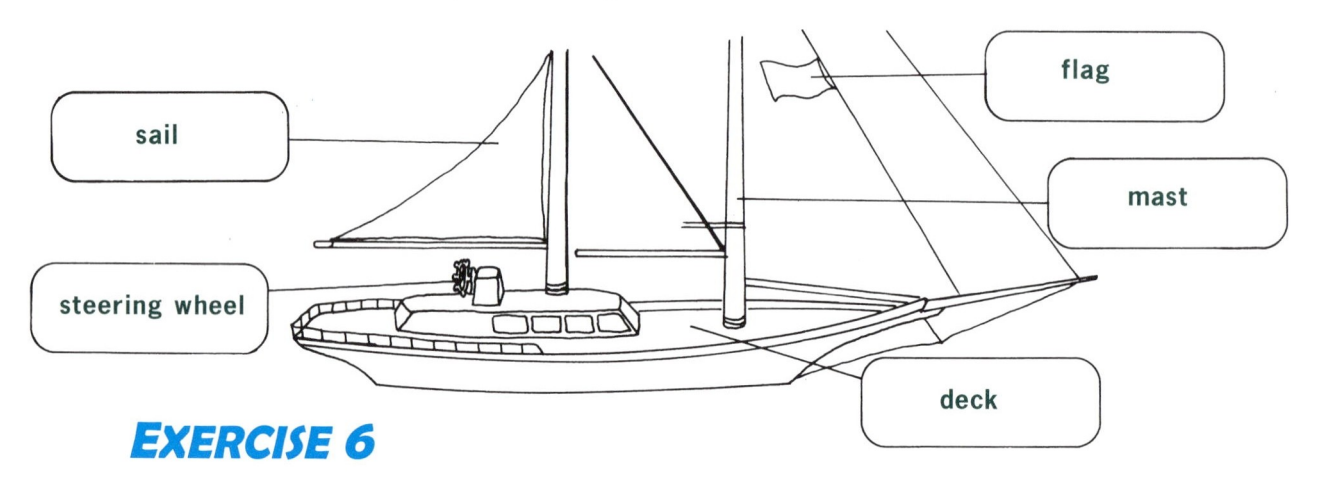

- sail
- flag
- mast
- steering wheel
- deck

EXERCISE 6

Do you know of any myths or legends connected with the sea? Read the account of the mermaid below and then complete the exercise which follows it:

The Mermaid

Mermaids appear in the oldest legends of some of the world's oldest cultures. Sailors returning from far-off lands and seas often spoke of seeing mermaids and 'sea wives'. Alexander the Great, it was said, had several adventures with beautiful sea maidens, visiting the bottom of the sea in a glass globe. According to myth, mermaids have no soul and in folk tradition they are sad and lonely creatures. One story tells of the beautiful mermaid of the Holy Island of Iona, off Scotland, who visited daily an unknown saint who lived there. She was in love with him and wanted the soul that mermaids lack. The saint told her that, to gain a soul, she must renounce the sea. This was impossible, so she left in despair and never returned. But her tears remained and form the grey-green pebbles which are found only on the island.

Look up the meanings of these words if you don't know them and then complete the sentences below:

| lack | globe | renounce | legend | myth | tradition |

1 In keeping with ____tradition____ , we decided to have turkey for our Christmas dinner.

2 The Geography teacher asked me to point out where Africa was on the __globe__ .

3 Your daughter should concentrate more on her schoolwork, Mrs Jacobs; she __lacks__ self-discipline.

4 Medusa was the unfortunate woman in the Greek __myth__ who was loved by the god of the sea.

5 I remember reading about the __legend__ of Robin Hood when I was a small child.

6 When Max Muggins the Mugger was released from jail he decided to __renounce__ his previous way of life and become a monk.

EXERCISE 7

Use the word 'fish' to form compound nouns in order to identify the items below:

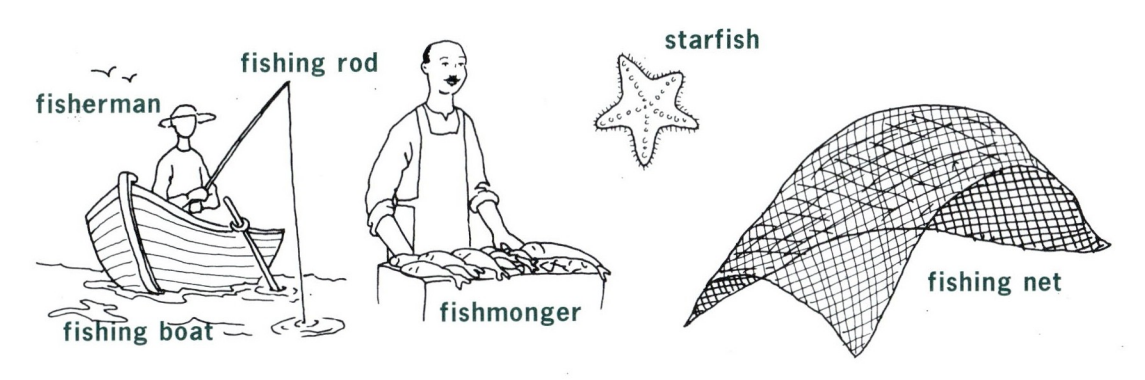

- fisherman
- fishing rod
- starfish
- fishing boat
- fishmonger
- fishing net

Complete the sentences with the words above:

1 Someone who sells fish in a shop is called a __fishmonger__ .

2 A flat sea creature with five arms is a __starfish__ .

3 The men took a small __fishing boat__ out to sea for the morning catch.

4 An old man was sitting on the harbour wall, mending his __fishing net__ with nylon thread.

5 Uncle Jack showed me how to hold the __fishing rod__ and told me I had to be very quiet and very patient if I wanted to catch a fish.

6 A bearded __fisherman__ entertained the sailors with his tales of past adventures at sea.

sport & fitness

EXERCISE 1

Sports venues

Where might the following sports be played?

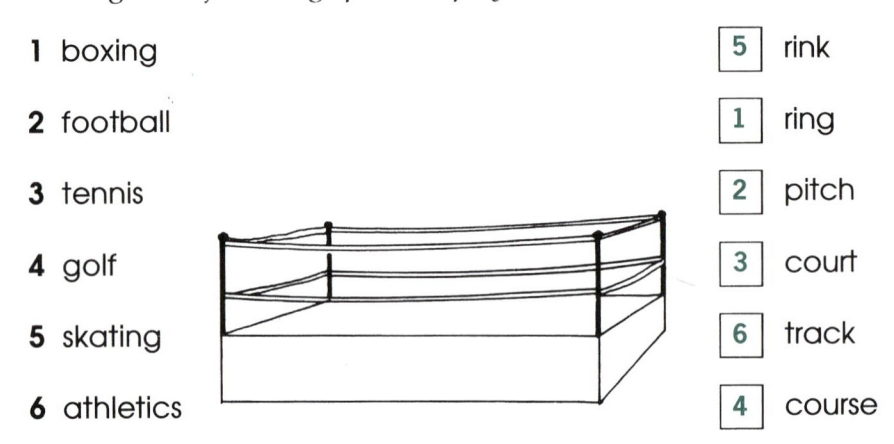

1 boxing
2 football
3 tennis
4 golf
5 skating
6 athletics

5	rink
1	ring
2	pitch
3	court
6	track
4	course

Complete the sentences below with any of the venues mentioned either above or in the box below:

> ground   stadium   field

1 Concerts are sometimes held in the Olympic __stadium__

2 The first time I played tennis, I couldn't even keep the ball inside the __court__ .

3 The football match was postponed because the __pitch__ was waterlogged.

4 Athletics consists of track and __field__ sports such as running, the high jump, the javelin, etc.

5 The team felt at an advantage since they were playing (on their) home __ground__

60

EXERCISE 2

Many team sports involve hitting a ball. Match the following pieces of equipment with the sport in which each is used:

1 stick

2 club

3 racquet

4 bat

4	cricket
3	tennis
1	hockey
2	golf

EXERCISE 3

Scoring

Match the sport with the scoring system used:

1 tennis

2 football

3 cricket

4 rugby

5 boxing

4	try
3	run
5	round
2	goal
1	point

EXERCISE 4

Which sports do you associate with the following expressions?

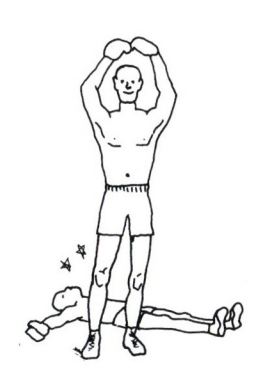

EXPRESSIONS	SPORTS
knock-out	boxing
hole in one	golf
bull's-eye	archery, darts
hat trick	football, cricket

61

EXERCISE 5

Ways of opening a game

Match the following ways with the appropriate sport:

1 tennis
2 football
3 cricket
4 golf

[4] tee-off
[3] bat
[1] serve
[2] kick-off

EXERCISE 6

Movements

Fill the gaps in the sentences below using the verbs given in the box:

| bend | stretch | climb | lean | push |

1 The average housewife has to ___climb___ the stairs about 22 times a day.

2 Don't ___lean___ against that window; it's not very safe.

3 To do this exercise, you have to ___bend___ from the hips and touch your toes.

4 We had to ___push___ the car to the side of the road and wait for the mechanic to arrive.

5 If you stand on tiptoe and ___stretch___ your body upwards, you might be able to touch the ceiling.

EXERCISE 7

☞ Eating habits are gradually changing. Doctors and nutrition experts are encouraging people to eat less red meat, less sugar and more fresh vegetables.
Below are five words connected with eating:.

DIET   VEGETARIAN   WHOLEFOOD   ADDITIVES   ENERGY

☞ People have more time to spare these days, so many take up exercise as a hobby. With excess energy needing to be used up, fitness and health have become popular interests. Below are five common words related to exercising.

JOGGING   GYMNASTICS   WORKOUT   AEROBICS   KEEP FIT

Find these 10 words in the wordsearch square below:

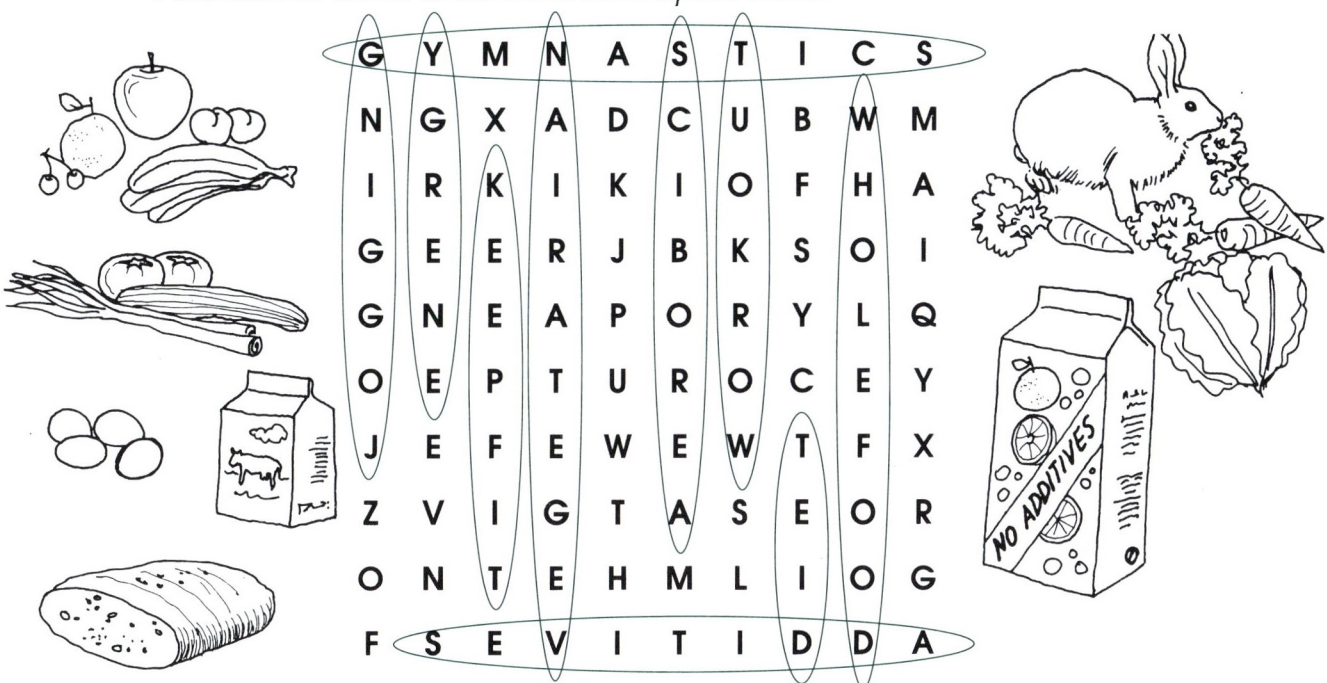

G	Y	M	N	A	S	T	I	C	S
N	G	X	A	D	C	U	B	W	M
I	R	K	I	K	I	O	F	H	A
G	E	E	R	J	B	K	S	O	I
G	N	E	A	P	O	R	Y	L	Q
O	E	P	T	U	R	O	C	E	Y
J	E	F	E	W	E	W	T	F	X
Z	V	I	G	T	A	S	E	O	R
O	N	T	E	H	M	L	I	O	G
F	S	E	V	I	T	I	D	D	A

63